Howard Agnew Johnston

Moses and the Pentateuch

A Popular Statement of the Theories of the So-Called Higher Criticism

Howard Agnew Johnston

Moses and the Pentateuch
A Popular Statement of the Theories of the So-Called Higher Criticism

ISBN/EAN: 9783337159498

Printed in Europe, USA, Canada, Australia, Japan

Cover: Foto ©Lupo / pixelio.de

More available books at **www.hansebooks.com**

MOSES

AND THE PENTATEUCH.

A POPULAR STATEMENT OF THE THEORIES
OF THE SO-CALLED HIGHER CRITICISM,
TOGETHER WITH SOME OF THE
REASONS FOR NOT AC-
CEPTING THEM

BY

Rev. Howard Agnew Johnston, Ph.D.

*Pastor of the Forty-first Street Presbyterian
Church, Chicago.*

CINCINNATI, O.:
Elm Street Printing Co., Nos. 176 and 178 Elm St.

CONTENTS.

Chapter.	Page.
I. Introductory,	5
II. Some Leading Critics, and What We Might Expect of Them,	11
III. The Development of the Theory and the Disagreement of the Critics Among Themselves,	17
IV. The Main Arguments Presented by the Critics Against the Mosaic Authorship, with Answers to the Same,	26
V. The Main Arguments in Favor of the Mosaic Authorship,	35
VI. Recent Corroborative Discoveries from the Monuments,	43
VII. The Book of Genesis,	52
VIII. The Book of Exodus,	58
IX. The Book of Leviticus,	64
X. The Book of Numbers,	70
XI. The Book of Deuteronomy,	78
XII. The Book of Joshua and the Term "Hexateuch,"	86
XIII. A Word About Alleged Errors and Existing Discrepancies,	93
XIV. Christ and the Critics,	100
XV. Concluding Remarks,	111

PUBLISHERS' NOTE.

The contents of this volume appeared in a series of articles in the *Herald and Presbyter*. In answer to many requests, they are presented to the public in this permanent form, with appropriate changes in the introductory chapter. The original form will explain a variety of features that are left unchanged. By arrangement the chapters are brief and concise, rather than comprehensive.

I.—INTRODUCTORY.

The writer of this little book is the pastor of a large congregation of busy people. Frequent inquiries from some of these people have been made concerning the theories of the higher criticism. The fact has developed that the publications which present the subject are of a technical character, and intended mainly for specialists. And so it has seemed to the writer that many Bible students who have no access to the sources of special information would be glad to have a popular statement of the theories and methods of higher criticism, especially if they should be accompanied by the reasons which lead the great majority of Christians to reject the conclusions reached and the methods applied. Such a statement is proposed in this volume. A glance at the table of contents will reveal the purpose to set forth the historic setting of the movement, and its salient features. It has been impossible to do more than state briefly, the views for and against the theory, but it is hoped that this brevity will not be at the expense of fairness and clearness.

It will be noted that according to the scope of the plan a general consideration of the subject will be followed by a particular examination of the problems that arise in each book. This will at once simplify and clarify the work, for each book has problems peculiar to itself, especially in the case of Genesis and Deuteronomy. Exodus has a striking unity, though Leviticus and Numbers are closely bound to it. At the start we shall present a few biographical items which will make it clear why some of the most famous of the critics have revealed such avidity in attempting to destroy the Christian's confidence in the word of God. We may not impugn the sincerity of the evangelical Christian who follows in the wake of the critics who are avowed Unitarians and Agnostics; but as we note the views of these leaders who repudiate miracle and prophecy and inspiration itself, we can not but feel that it is time for evangelical Christians to stand out against them. The best way to do this is not to dismiss the subject by calling them heretics; but to present fairly their views and show wherein they fail of a legitimate claim upon the adherence of the Christian.

The simple fact is that the higher criticism is not only dangerous and destructive, but it is also unscientific. Exact science makes a twofold demand. It makes necessary the cutting of the bridge of tradition. No less imperative is the obligation which it lays upon the careful student to refuse to bridge over theories which lack demonstration, however fascinating and popular. True science suffers in both of these directions. The progressive unfolding of new phases of the truth is crippled in part because some people cling with unreasonable and unreasoning prejudice to traditional views which clearly ascertained facts have proven untenable. No doubt, one reason for this is the rash, unscientific haste with which the champions of new theories put them forth as worthy of acceptance, when they are far from demonstration. If the student desires to investigate some samples of colossal conjecture and astounding assumption, let him study some of the theories of the higher criticism. Some of those theories, as, for instance, the number of editings which the Pentateuch has undergone, are absolutely without a shadow of conclusive evidence.

We are told the world's greatest scholars are advocates and supporters of the higher criticism. But what makes a great scholar? Not inventive ingenuity in theorizing; not keen analytical power of itself. If these lack a steadfast level-headedness and fidelity to facts, a prime element in scholarship is missing. It is true that the race has witnessed more than one mighty intellect burn out in dreaming about some scheme of philosophy or criticism which has never helped us one inch toward the truth. One who toils through much of the marvelously painstaking labors of many of these gifted men can not but think of Longfellow's description in "Hyperion" of much of the German philosophy. He said it reminded him of a pleasant street in one of our American towns, where it, at first, was wide and attractive, lined with beautiful trees; but which ran out into the country, losing its importance, until at last it dwindled into a squirrel track and ran up a tree. We will prize scholarship by what it gives us at the last. Just as capable and scholarly men repudiate the essential teachings of the higher criticism as are found among their advocates. It could not be otherwise with their theories assailable at every point.

It is time for conservative Christian scholarship to speak with less apologetic tone in defense of the substantial Mosaic authorship of the Pentateuch. The higher criticism has been given a hearing, but has failed signally to establish the destructive views which it has striven to propagate. This failure is becoming more apparent in the light of recent monumental discoveries. This vast field of modern science has been ignored by the critics to their hurt. Our plan includes some account of these findings and their testimony against the fundamental assumption of higher criticism. In the course of this presentation, constant reference will be given to the authorities cited on both sides, so that one so desiring can follow up the subject to the extent of his inclination. The writer is of those who desire full place for the truth, no matter what preconceived notion may be set aside; but who refuse to set aside accepted views until fair demonstration demands it. Let us "prove all things," and 'hold fast that which is good."

II.—Some Leading Critics and What We Might Expect of Them.

Much light is thrown upon the significance of the higher criticism when we consider the theological views in general of the leading critics. It is impossible to cut between a man's general attitude toward the word of God and his critical theories. We can not fail to see that a rationalist who rejects miracle, prophecy and inspiration, would bring a purely naturalistic theory to an examination of the Scriptures. The historic fact is that the conspicuous leaders among the critics have been rationalists, and a delicate sensitiveness to the truth can not be divested of the feeling that their theories are the product, not so much of an honest seeking for the truth, as of a desire to destroy the evangelical faith by the constraint involved in the claim of scientific scholarship.

In proof of this we have the following statement concerning Dr. Abraham Kuenen in the

Jewish Quarterly Review: "It was an attempt of singular boldness and vigor to shake the tradition of Christian piety free from every trace of supernaturalism and implied exclusiveness. It involved the absolute surrender of the orthodox dogmatics, of the authority of the Scriptures, of the divine character of the Church as an external institution, and, of course, it based the claims of Jesus of Nazareth to our affection and gratitude solely upon what history could show that he, as a man, had been and had done for men."—*Wickstead, Jewish Quarterly Review,* July, 1892. And this is exactly what we would expect of a Jewish scholar. We may not question his convictions as sincere, as we may not question the honesty of any Unitarian's convictions. But no more can the evangelical Christian expect to find a common ground with such men for reverent criticism of the word of God.

A list of higher critics is given us by Dr. Charles A. Briggs in an appendix to his book on "The Bible, the Church and the Reason." This list contains 147 names; seventeen of this number are Jews and five are Unitarians.

Thirty, at least, of the whole number do not believe in the supernatural in the Bible at all, while many more hold decidedly loose ideas of inspiration. Canon Driver defines inspiration as "spiritual insight," and nothing more. Now, it is true that these rationalist and rationalistic men are the leaders of the higher criticism. It is equally true that of the hundred or more followers of these leaders, those who have gone to any length in adopting the critical views have betrayed in their writings clear tendencies to rationalism. It is also true that the students of these critics betray a tendency toward naturalistic grounds in their opinions touching related lines of thought. More than once the writer has verified this fact in conversation with men from the class-room of German and American teachers.

When, therefore, the critics parade the names of Tuch, Knobel, De Wette, Bohlen, Bleek, Ewald, Delitzsch, Graf, Kuenen, Wellhausen, Dillman and others, we can not consent to be carried away by such a flourish of trumpets, for the work which we have in hand is not a matter to be determined for evangelical Christendom by any number of brilliant intellects. Dr. Briggs mentions Ernest Renan in his list of critics. Had he not restricted his list, he might also have mentioned Francois Voltaire, as he also advocated the very same views concerning the Mosaic authorship of the Pentateuch. When we think of the subtle infidelity of Renan, in his ineffective endeavor to stab to the heart the evangelical faith, we are startled indeed to have Dr. Briggs tell us that evangelical scholarship must yield to a class of men with whom Ernest Renan is in accord in the cardinal points of their destructive criticism. Is it not time to call a halt along this line?

Of course, it is not asserted that because a man is an infidel or a rationalist, he may not be an honest student of history or of literature, from his standpoint. But the difficulty is with his standpoint. It is nothing less than absurd to expect a man who denies the possibility of the miracles recorded in the Old Testament, and who denies the possibility of an inspiration by which men were led to predict future events, to enter upon a study of the Old Testament history and literature without being destructive of the very foundations of faith in the Bible as the word of God. But just such men are the leaders of this critical development. It need not be argued here that evangelical Christians can not expect light from such sources, nor need it be argued that we must guard the more earnestly against the subtle encroachments which the enemies of what we believe to be the saving truth of God would fain make upon our faith.

It is not to be denied that the critics have a following among evangelical scholars. But it is to be noted that those who are at all enthusiastic in their adherence to the critical methods clearly betray naturalistic tendencies in their writings. Over against these are to be mentioned some of the strongest men in the realm of modern scholarship. Among them are Hengstenberg, Haeverinck, Keil, Sayce, Green, DeWitt, Osgood, Bissell and W. J. Beecher. These men stand for the divine character of the Bible as against the theory of its human production. They stand for the substantial Mosaic authorship of the Pentateuch. They are scholars of equal ability in discerning a fair demonstration of any theory touching the Old Testament writings with any of the critics. They are open to the truth, ready to be convinced by any reasonable demonstration; but entirely unwilling to shut their eyes to the insuperable barriers that thus far stand in the way of the unscientific processes of the critics. It is further true that there are some men counted as critics who, to say the least, are half-hearted supporters of the analysis. Prof. W. R. Harper is continually confessing difficulties that arise upon which the critics can throw no light.

In view of these facts it will not be surprising to find the theories of the critics, which we shall now proceed to consider, of such character as they are. Nor will we be surprised that so many reject these theories, as we note the reason for not accepting them. Evangelical scholars meet the critics at every point, showing the weakness and insufficiency of their views.

III.—The Development of the Theory and the Disagreement of the Critics Among Themselves.

Prior to the last century, the substantial Mosaic authorship of the Pentateuch was conceded by almost the unanimous voice of Hebrew and Christian scholarship. The exceptions were inconspicuous, and occurred mainly in the second century. Epiphanius tells us an obscure party of Nazarenes considered the present Pentateuch as spurious The Gnostic Ptolemaeus ascribed only a portion of the work to Moses. The Clementine Homilies suggest that because the account of the death of Moses occurs at the end of the work, Moses did not write any of it. Attempts have been made by the critics to show that Jerome in the fourth century, and Aben Ezra in the twelfth century, discredited the Mosaic authorship. But this can not fairly be done. Jerome simply says he does not object to the idea of a post-exilian revision, and Aben Ezra does nothing more than intimate that subsequent interpolations had crept into the original text.

In the year 1651, the English deist, Thomas Hobbes, published his "Leviathan," in which he assailed the Mosaic authorship. The idea was taken up by the deistic philosophers of the latter half of the seventeenth century, notably Shaftesbury and Bolingbroke, both of whom were practical atheists, while the latter's immorality is known to history. About the same time, Spinoza in Holland, and Richard Simon in France, advocated the same view with variations. Both of these men were Jews of a most pronounced rationalistic type of thought. Spinoza's philosophy was denounced in his day as systematic atheism. David Hume, the English skeptic, was his admiring pupil. Spinoza abhorred the traditional theology, and did all in his power to rationalize the interpretation of the Old Testament. The names of Vitringa and Laclerc should also be mentioned, as they gave some impetus to the theory at the end of the seventeenth century and the beginning of the eighteenth.

In the early half of the last century, Dr. Herman Samuel Reimarus, of Hamburg, elaborated the theory at some length. Professor Pfleiderer, of Berlin, says of him: "Reimarus, the author of the 'Wolfenbuttel Fragments,' by the publication of which Lessing threw German theology into a ferment, occupies the same position as the English deists, and indeed owed much to their influence." At the same time the man who was dominating the popular thought of France was Voltaire. The extent of his influence upon all classes is simply amazing to us of to-day. Spinoza and the English deists were his delight. Of the latter he said: "Many of these have advanced so far as to doubt whether Moses ever existed." Such are the actual hotbeds of rationalism in which the seeds of modern higher criticism had root. Professor Osgood clearly puts the attitude of these men toward the Bible, as denying that it was in any sense from God or a revelation of religion; that it was anything else than a "growth and compilation, in accordance with the ordinary laws, and subject to the ordinary errors of the human mind.' If we should be accused of unfair prejudice in these statements, we need but to refer to the following extract from

Kuenen, in his work on the Prophets: "So long as we derive a separate part of Israel's religious life directly from God, and allow the supernatural or immediate revelation to intervene in even one single point, so long also our view of the whole continues to be incorrect. It is the supposition of a natural development alone which accounts for all the phenomena." Could the fruit be any more like the seed? It simply means that radical higher criticism would destroy utterly the divine character of the Bible.

In the year 1753, Dr. Jean Astruc, an eminent Belgian physician, published a book at Brussels, entitled "Conjectures About the Original Memoirs which Moses Used in Composing the Book of Genesis." In this treatise Astruc suggested that Moses compiled the Book of Genesis largely from pre-existing materials. This he thought apparent, because of the way the two names for God—Elohim and Jehovah—were used. Most Bible students not familiar with the Hebrew are aware that there are different names of God used in the text, two of them much more than the rest. They are El, or Elohim, translated God in the

English, and Javeh, vocalized in our text into Jehovah. There are sections in Genesis where now one, now another, of these terms is used, and to such an extent as to suggest that the sections were written by different men, one of whom at least was familiar with but one of these words. Astruc conjectured that Moses had used twelve pre-existing documents, two principal ones and ten others. Professor Eichhorn pruned off some of Astruc's conjectures and confined his theory to the advocacy of two documents. Some of his contemporaries, as Illgen and Gramberg, advocated three documents.

But this documentary hypothesis was quite too conservative for some of the critics. In 1815 Dr. Johann Severin Vater gave out the more startling theory that the Pentateuch consisted merely of a number of fragments strung together without order or design. He supposed a collection of laws made at the time of David and Solomon to have been the foundation of the whole; that this was the lost book found in the days of Josiah, its fragments being incorporated into the Book of Deuteronomy. The rest of the Pentateuch consists of fragments of tradition, history and law collected into form between the reign of Josiah and the Babylonian exile. Dr. A. T. Hartmann was in accord with Vater's theory. But this fragment-hypothesis has been almost universally abandoned by later critics. Even DeWette, who held to it for a time, has relinquished it for the earlier documentary hypothesis to which modern critics have returned. Most of these assert that there are evidences of at least four original documents. These are said to be (1) an earlier Elohistic document, known as the priest code, and indicated by the letter P; (2) the Jehovistic document, indicated by the letter J; (3) a later Elohistic document, indicated by the letter E. Theories vary about the fourth element; some claim to detect an earlier writer in J, known as J^1. Besides, credit is given to editors, redactors and glosses.

In the next chapter we shall enter upon a more detailed statement of the general argument for these theories, and afterwards we shall consider more specifically each separate book in turn. The very important discrimination to be made here touches the fact that the Mosaic authorship of the Pentateuch, while it makes impossible the assumed later compilation, does not make impossible the use of pre-existing materials by Moses himself, nor an arrangement of the whole in its present form at a later date. The critics would blot out Moses, but give us no one in his place. They announce that the various authors are unknown. The fact is, these authors come out of the theory. The book is divided up into sections, and the theory demands authors for the same, and lo! P. and J. and E. spring Minerva-like from the Jovian brain of the critics. But no such artificial dissection will win final recognition, simply because the character of Moses can not be effaced from the Pentateuch. It breathes that potent spirit of living contemporaneous history which defies the *ex post facto* explanation of the critics. Not only so, but the theory is met by stubborn facts at almost every point, as will appear in our further treatment of the case.

The critics have largely vitiated their own attempts to make a case by their disagreements among themselves. Not only is the analysis in general marked by frequently recurring inconsistencies, but the different views and sharp contentions of the critics lead many to ask, with Dr. Green, which one we may accept as authority. In the account of the development of the theory this fact of difference in view has appeared But as the detailed study of the text is taken up, the reader is bewildered by finding one critic positively assigning a given passage to P., while another as positively assigns it to J. Kuenen actually asserts that there have been fifteen redactors, editing and re-editing the work. All this, we are told, is the result of the most exact scientific processes. Then, behold! Wellhausen comes after Kuenen with nineteen redactors, and departs from Kuenen because his position was "polytheism and monotheism together." We have charged the higher criticism with being unscientific. Certainly no demonstrable science would ever plunge the student into such a labyrinth of hopeless contradictions and fanciful conjectures. Every one desiring to see the most valuable presentation of the theory in all its startling and almost incredible character should by all means examine the work of Prof. E. C. Bissell entitled "Genesis Printed in Colors." By selecting a special color to represent each assumed document, and various col ors to indicate glosses and the work of redactors, Dr. Bissell presents to the mind through the eye the result of the analysis as adopted by Kautzch and Socin. An exceedingly valuable introduction precedes the work. If a copy of this book could be placed in the hands of every unprejudiced Bible student, the hopeless doom of higher criticism would be settled within sixty days.

IV.—The Main Arguments Presented by the Critics against the Mosaic Authorship, with Answers to the Same.

Before entering upon the statement of these arguments, the fact should be emphasized that the claim for the Mosaic authorship does not preclude the use by Moses of pre existent materials. Probably no one would question the probability of such use. The institutions of the Sabbath and circumcision existed before the time of Moses. The events chronicled in the Book of Genesis antedate the time of Moses We shall see later on that the monuments furnish conclusive evidence of the existence of such materials as would be available in part for the work which Moses was commanded to accomplish. Some of the critics concede parts of the Pentateuch to the hand of Moses, especially the laws in Deuteronomy. But the critics deny that the substantial contents of the Pentateuch are to be credited to him. Dr. Briggs reiterated in his defense the following statement from his inaugural: "It may be regarded as the certain result of the science of the higher criticism that Moses did not write the Pentateuch. . . . The great mass of the Old Testament was written by authors whose names or connection with their writings are lost in oblivion." In proof of this the critics rest mainly upon the following arguments:

1. It is asserted that the structure of the narrative betrays a composite character. The earlier theories suggested this concerning Genesis alone, as in the "conjectures" of Astruc, but now it is urged that the Elohistic and Jehovistic writings can be traced through the whole book. To prove this point it is urged (1) that there are irreconcilable differences in the two parts of the narrative which describe the same event. An instance is the twofold account of the creation in Gen. i. 2, 3, and ii 4–25 Others are the accounts of the flood, the story of the exodus, the number of the feasts, the sending of the quails and the murmuring for water. (2) The fact is also urged in proof of composite authorship that the same account is repeated, as in the com-

mand for the national festivals (Exod. xvii. 1-7, and xxxiv. 23-26), as also in the penal statutes for the violations of the marriage laws (Lev. xviii. xx). (3) It is claimed further that the Elohist has a range of simpler ideas than the Jehovist, who is more elaborate in vocabulary and style. (4) Moreover, it is claimed that these writers have certain favorite expressions and pet phrases which distinguish them. For instance, they tell us the Elohist will say to *give* or *establish* a covenant, while the Jehovist will say to *cut* a covenant. The Jehovist also has credited to him grammatical peculiarities, as the use of the infinitive absolute for the sake of emphasis. (5) The claim is also made that Exod. vi. 2 indicates that the name Jehovah was not revealed until the time of Moses. How this could be urged against the Mosaic authorship does not appear.

In answer to the above assertions, it may be said (1) that the unity of the Pentateuch as a whole is too palpable to be denied, but the critics say this is not because its present form came mainly from one author, but because some later writer worked up the various parts into this unity. The fact is, however, that only the most arbitrary suppositions and inexplicable gaps make it possible to call the narrative a reconstruction of fragments. This fact will be more fully elaborated in considering the Book of Genesis in chapter vii. Moreover, the critics are in hopeless disagreement as to what exactly constitutes each original part. As to the time of the literary genius who gave us the present form, Stahelin fixes it at the time of Saul; DeWette, Knobel and Bleek at the time of Josiah; Kuenen at the end of the seventh century B. C.; Ewald before the destruction of Jerusalem; Hartmann, Bohlen and Wellhausen after the exile. They each tell us they reach these conclusions by strictly scientific processes. (2) As to the alleged contradictions, without exception they may be easily explained by the exercise of ordinary common sense. As a rule the items are clearly supplementary, and not contradictory. (3) The repetitions mentioned have distinct features. Lev. xviii. commands family purity. Chapter xx. contains some of the same commands under an elaboration of the Decalogue. In any case, to assert a fundamental composite authorship because of these infrequent repetitions is quite without warrant. (4) As to the linguistic peculiarities, Keil says in the first volume of his introduction: "We everywhere discover a difference in the conception which is demanded by the sense and context of the individual passages, or else the peculiar words ascribed to the one author are really not unknown to the other, or they occur in a few solitary places, and therefore are not entitled to be considered characteristic." (5) The notion that the name Jehovah was not known before Moses suggests a failure to have noted it in utterances of the patriarchs, as in Gen. iv. 1, v. 29; ix. 26; xiv. 22; xx. 4, etc.

2. It is asserted that the contents of the books are unhistorical in character. (1) A few years ago it was argued quite confidently that the Egyptology of the Pentateuch was so full of errors as to have made it impossible for Moses to have written it. Bohlen especially urged this view. It may be briefly stated that a dead and buried Egypt, of which Herodotus never knew, has uncovered her sepulchres and risen up to refute every single

charge of the critics. We have the testimony of Rawlinson, in his Historical Illustrations of the Old Testament, "that in the entire Mosaic description of ancient Egypt there is not a single feature which is out of harmony with what we know of the Egypt of this remote period from other sources." (2) A second specification under this charge asserts the inaccurate character of much of the geographical, chronological and arithmetical statements. It is true that in the realm of figures, both in dates and numbers, it is difficult to find exact harmony. This fact, however, does not make against any particular author. Reasonable explanations are given for almost every point. As to the geography, the remarkable fact stands that the list of camping-places given in Num. xxxiii., and said to contain errors, is conceded by the critics to be one of the indubitable Mosaic fragments. (3) One other charge is made against the historic reliability of the book, which does not stop at the point of authorship. Kuenen says the record of miracles and certain other incidents are simply mythological legends. This, of course, denies divine inspiration, and we need not here do more than state it to the evangelical reader.

3. The critics tell us that the literature of a people must have a natural development; that the Hebrews, at the exodus, were a race of slaves, and that the Pentateuch could not have been the production of that age. This theory is in accord with the naturalistic attitude which they bring to the study of the book. The very facts mentioned point to Moses as the only possible author of the book, for he was a prince in the palace and learned in all the wisdom of the Egyptians. More important, however, is the testimony of the monuments in proof of the literary activity among the Semitic peoples previous to the time of Moses. The critics assume a literary renaissance of the restoration, yet Gesenius declares Ezra, Nehemiah, Esther and Chronicles to be inferior literary work. The theory here simply goes down before facts.

4. It is urged that the resemblance of the language of the Pentateuch to that of later books argues for its later authorship. Especially is this resemblance urged between Deuteronomy and Jeremiah. In our chapter

on Deuteronomy we shall consider this resemblance. In general it may be said that Jeremiah shows great familiarity with the other books of the Pentateuch, as well as with Deuteronomy. Further, it may be said that whatever resemblance may be noticed is offset by a decided diversity, not only in contents, but in literary style. It may be said just here that a little patient study of the text reveals such a constant reference to the Pentateuch in almost every succeeding book of the Old Testament as to prove its earlier existence according to the generally accepted rules of scientific literary criticism.

5. The critics assert there are traces of a later date, indicating the age in which the author lived. (1) Passages which seem to presuppose the occupation of the land, as Gen. xxxvi 31. This statement is said to indicate the time of the monarchy, but it must be remembered that in Gen. xxxv. 11, kings are promised to Israel, and this is but a statement of developments previous to that anticipated time. (2) Passages which seem to imply the Palestinian standpoint of the author, as Gen. xii. 8. (3) Passages which explain archaic

usages and terms by those of a later origin, as Gen. xiv. 2, "Bela, which is Zoar." It need only be said that the later names were known in the time of Moses. (4) Citations from documents of recognized antiquity, as Num. xxi. 14, where reference is made to the Book of the Wars of Jehovah. But it is simply an assumption to say this book was of recognized antiquity Nothing prevents its having been contemporaneous, so far as the record is concerned. (5) Passages which contain the formula "unto this day," as Gen. xix. 37. None of the instances require an explanation beyond the fact that the phrase partakes of the nature of a proverbial expression designed to represent an event or transaction as of permanent character. In short, no theory of the critics against the substantial Mosaic authorship has any ground for a fair demonstration. All of them are open to strong legitimate objection and some of them are met with clear refutation.

V.—The Main Arguments in Favor of the Mosaic Authorship.

The reader of these articles will realize that we are attempting to make a reasonably adequate statement of views in defense of which volumes have been written. Brevity here is at the risk of obscurity, but it is hoped that any one especially interested will enter upon a more extended investigation of the subject. We can but indicate the salient points on either side of the controversy. Under the topic for this chapter there are several lines of argument.

1. On its face the Pentateuch carries a clear presumption in favor of the Mosaic authorship. There is the direct testimony of the Book to this effect in Ex. xvii. 14 and xxiv. 3-7; Num. xxxiii. 1, 2; Deut. xvii. 18, 19, a remarkable passage; mention of *written* blessings and curses in Deut. xxviii. and xxx, xxvii. 1-13, and most notable of all, Deut. xxxi. 9-13; xxiv. 27. Add to this the warning

against adding to or taking from what Moses commanded, Deut. iv. 2; xii. 32. Note also Num. xxxvi. 13 and Lev. xxv. 1; xxvi 46; xxvii. 34. Almost on entering the wilderness the Hebrew lawgiver received a divine order to write in the Book. On reaching Sinai he is discovered again writing in the Book of the Covenant. As the wanderings in the wilderness were nearing their termination, he is stated to have prepared a written record of the halting-places in the march. And just before he dies he is once more writing "this book of the law." If ever there was a *prima-facie* inference, it is here to the effect that Moses was the substantial author of the Pentateuch.

2. It was possible for Moses to have written it. A few years ago some of the critics urged that there were no Semitic writers prior to 1,000 B.C. Of course, all that is now given up—for we shall see in the next chapter that the monuments have proved not only the knowledge of the art of writing in the time of Moses, but the existence of records at the time of Abraham, giving accounts of primitive history, which seem to have been handed

down from the earliest times. As to the material found in Exodus and Deuteronomy inclusive, it must have been available for Moses as for no one else. It is further true that the Mosaic authorship will account for the accurate and minute details which everywhere appear in a knowledge of Egypt and the desert life.

3. The Mosaic authorship is necessary to an adequate explanation of the historic development of the national life of the Hebrews. Suddenly these people took their place among the settled nations and entered upon that conspicuous and unique racial development which has continued even to this day. While there were acknowledged affinities in some points with contiguous nations, it must be ad mitted that their whole system was sharply separated by the grandeur of its religious monotheism, and by its complex social and civil organization, from that of all other nations. Their code of laws was so penetrating as to impress its indelible peculiarities upon the race, and to endow it with a potency and perpetuity of national life, in the face of terrific counter influences, to which history fur-

nishes no parallel. Such an effect demands a cause; and that cause is the living system known as Mosaism. As the New Testament Church is inconceivable without the incarnation of Christ and the apostolic Gospels, so the Old Testament Church is inconceivable without a Sinaitic revelation and a Mosaic Pentateuch.

4. It is simply incredible that some "great Unknown" should have foisted upon the people of Israel at any date later than Moses this book which was credited to him by the people. Dr. Bleek admits that in the time of Christ it was the universal belief that Moses was the author of the entire Pentateuch. Josephus says: "All our constitution depends on Moses our legislator. For we have not an innumerable multitude of books, disagreeing from and contradicting one another (as the Greeks have), but only twenty-two books, which contain the records of all past times, which are justly claimed to be divine, and of them five belong to Moses, which contain his laws and the tradition of the origin of mankind until his death." Philo says: "We find that in the sacred oracles delivered

by the prophet Moses, there are three kinds of characters; for a portion of them relates to the creation of the world a portion is historical, and a third portion is legislative." These testimonies reflect the accepted view of all Jews. Pharisees, Sadducees, Essenes, Palestinian and Alexandrian Jews all are agreed on this point. To suppose that such a view would be universal if the Pentateuch had been given to the people at any time after the division of the monarchy, is to charge the Jewish people with a lack of intelligence and a weakness of credulity utterly unworthy of their history. The critics would have us believe the imagined Unknown first borrowed the name of Moses because of its superlative prestige, and then proceeded to re-enact the legislation of Moses in a broader and more spiritual manner, and with true prophetic inspiration. That is to say, they would have us believe that a greater than Moses arose in Israel, but sank out of sight without ever being recognized by his contemporaries, yet giving to his race the most important literary production in all their history, though his name has not a whisper of connection with it.

The credulity of the critics may be equal to this, but not many will be their followers.

5. A side light is thrown upon the subject by the existence of a Samaritan Pentateuch. Most scholars do not attribute much importance to this fact, and yet when all the circumstances are considered, the fact is not without significance and importance. The Samaritans accepted no other books of the Hebrew Scriptures except the Pentateuch. Knowing their hostility to the Jews of the restoration, it is utterly incredible that they would have accepted the Pentateuch had it been a postexilian production. Unquestionably they believed that it was from Moses, and their acceptance of it points clearly to an established recognition of the Mosaic authorship of the book as it is, previous to the rupture of the kingdom. But such evidence simply points to the existence of the book from the time of Moses.

6. The remaining Old Testament Scriptures, which are among the older productions, bear witness to the previous existence of the Pentateuch by striking references to passages in the same. Often there are verbal coincidences

of expression so accurate as to indicate a written antecedent rather than oral tradition. Hengstenberg, in his work on the "Authenticity of the Pentateuch," has rendered most valuable service to the student along this line. The Book of Joshua is so full of these references that the critics have been compelled to declare that it also was written at the later date which they give to the Pentateuch. We shall discuss this further in Chapter XII. In the Book of Judges the refusal of Gideon to receive the crown of Israel indicates a knowledge of the Mosaic law upon the subject. The same may be said with reference to Samuel's unwillingness to elect a king. The critics argue that Israel did not have all of the law in that early day in the land, on the ground that the records show so many violations of it. But Bleek himself, in his introduction, is candid enough to admit that the fact that the laws were not observed is not sufficient proof that they did not exist. In the earlier prophets, Isaiah, Micah, Amos, Hosea, there are continual references to the Pentateuch. It is also true that the Hebrew Psalter, whenever compiled, is a "precious fruit of the religious life of Israel under the law, and requires for its understanding just such a national history and ecclesiastical system as are presented in the Pentateuchal books."

7. Our Lord Jesus Christ expressly certified the Mosaic authorship of the Pentateuch. In Chapter XIV. we shall consider more fully this fact. Suffice it now to say that while the critics would turn aside this whole matter by saying that Christ and the apostles accommodated themselves to the popular beliefs of their time, the subject is quite incapable of being thus summarily dismissed. Until recent years Christ's word was final authority in the Evangelical Christian Church, and to most of the members of that Church the word of the Son of God still stands as the ultimate decisive utterance of infallible truth.

VI.—Recent Corroborative Discoveries From the Monuments.

"One by one," says Professor Sayce, of Oxford, "the narratives of the Old Testament upon which the oversubtle analysis of modern criticism had cast suspicion and doubt are being vindicated by the progress of Oriental research." It should be said, moreover, that the critics have largely ignored this realm of scientific research. All along they have based one of their strongest arguments on the assumption that both the Israelites themselves and the populations by whom they were surrounded were ignorant of the art of writing books at the time of the conquest of Canaan and during the age of the judges. They supposed the literary period of Israel to have begun with Samuel. The oldest inscription yet discovered in the Phœnician alphabet is fixed at the time of the Moabite king Mesha, the contemporary of Ahab. The critics asked why no older inscriptions had been found, if the art of writing had been known centuries earlier. Within recent years the archæologist has given the answer. True, the earlier literature was not inscribed upon papyrus or written in forms of the Phœnician alphabet. It was entrusted to more enduring tablets of clay, while the language and script in which it has been preserved were both disused in the Palestine of a later day. A single blow of the excavator's pick has shattered some of the most ingenious conclusions of the critics.

Adhering to our plan of brief statements, we can only touch upon this fascinating subject. Every Bible student should be watching eagerly the result of the explorations which are being pushed in Egypt, Assyria and Palestine. The more familiar account of the Akkadian record of the flood is given by Professor Bissell, in his edition of Genesis, previously mentioned. This account is strikingly in accord with that in Genesis, especially in certain points attacked by the critics, as in the matter of a second announcement. Authorities agree that the date of the originals of this record is about 2000 B. C., or five hundred years before Moses. The Babylonian record is in the form of a simple continuous narrative which follows the biblical order. Thus the theory of the critics that the account in Genesis is made up of two fragmentary parts, and that it could not have been written in its present form by Moses, is set aside by the fact of its existence previous to Moses. To confirm the fact that Moses was familiar with this account, we have more recent dis coveries from the monuments which are of remarkable character in demonstrating great literary activity in Bible lands previous to the time of Moses.

In the year 1887-8 a number of cuneiform tablets were taken from the ruins of a city of ancient Egypt, the site of which is now known as Tel el-Amarna. They consist of letters and dispatches sent to the Egyptian court by the kings of Babylonia, Assyria and Syria, and the Egyptian governors and vassal princes in the subject province of Palestine. They are written in the script and language of Babylonia, which was at that time the common language of diplomacy, and it proves that there must have been a very general literary activity and some educational system to have mastered the complicated writing of Babylonia all through the East. The most interesting of the letters from Palestine are from a certain Ebed-Tob, the governor of Jerusalem. He was not governor by appointment of the king of Egypt, but an ally who paid tribute. He speaks of "the city of the mountain of Salim." The word "Uru" signified city, so that Urusalim is the city of Salim, identical with Jerusalem This Ebed-Tob speaks of himself as being a "priest of the most high God." We turn to Gen. xiv. and read the account of Melchizedek, king of Salem, priest of the most high God, and identify this description with that of the tablets, which thus carry us back to the time of Abraham. Not only so, but the "written bricks" confirm the account, in that same chapter of Genesis, of the incursion of Chedorlaomer, a Babylonian prince.

But the most remarkable coincidence in the history of this work occurred in the year 1892. Among the letters of the Tel el-Amarna tablets are two that were written by governors of the city of Lachish, one of whom was Zimrida. One of the letters from the king of Jerusalem conveys the information that Zimrida was murdered at Lachish by the servants of the Egyptian king. In 1890 Dr. Flinders Petrie was excavating in Southern Palestine, at a lofty mound known as Tel el Hesy. From various indications he suspected that he had identified this very city of Lachish. In 1892 the work was continued by Mr. Bliss, of Beirut. Not only did he fully identify the ancient Amorite city, but he found tablets exactly like those of Tel el-Amarna, and upon them this very name of Zimrida occurs twice. Scarcely have the letters from upper Egypt been translated, when their counterparts in Southern Palestine come to the light, and the two parts of a correspondence which took place before the Exodus are joined together. It is but the beginning, for Mr. Bliss is just at the entrance of the ancient archive chamber of the governor's palace.

The result of this recent discovery is conclusive evidence that the land of Canaan was inhabited by people who were by no means the unlettered tribes imagined by the critics. One of their cities was named Kirjath Sepher, which means "the city of books," and indicates libraries in Canaan as there were in

Babylonia. In the song of Deborah and Barak we read, in Judges v. 14, that "out of Zebulon came down they that handle the pen of the ready writer." This was clearly the Hebrew, but some other meaning was put into it, in the supposition that there were no ready writers. But the original text is now most clearly vindicated. Moreover, the tablets show that Canaan before the exodus was the great highway between the Mediterranean Sea and the eastern centers of commerce. Canaan paid to Egypt an annual land tax, which was assessed according to surveys of the Egyptian Government. The enlightened and warlike Amorites and Hittites were there, and many of the cities mentioned in the Scriptures are also mentioned on the tablets. Professor Maspero says: "The land of Canaan was a vast emporium where Africa met Europe and Asia." Professor Erman says: "There was hardly anything which the Egypt of the eighteenth and nineteenth dynasty had not obtained from Syria. The culture of the Syrians must therefore have been very highly advanced to have obtained such a conquest."

With all this information let it be remembered that the conquest by Israel was only partial even until the time of David. We are told in the first chapter of Judges that "the children of Benjamin did not drive out the Jebusites that inhabited Jerusalem, but the Jebusites dwell with the children of Benjamin in Jerusalem unto this day." We also read that Manasseh and Ephraim failed to dislodge the inhabitants of some six cities, while Zebulon, Asher, Naphtali and Dan failed to make their conquest complete. We know also how Israel grew into intimate relations with the people of the land, and whatever else they received of hurtful influences, we can not doubt that they must have felt the touch of their intellectual development and literary activity. Such was the literary atmosphere which pervaded the time when Moses wrote the Pentateuch. The increasing evidence from the monuments indicates that it was the golden age of literature in the history of the ancient East. Thus one of the strongest assumptions of the critics against the Mosaic authorship is completely annihilated.

We can not dismiss this brief mention without noting that the monuments have corroborated the Pentateuch in other ways, notably in confirming the accuracy of historic references. In May, 1890, Dr. Brugsch Bey wrote an article on "Joseph in Egypt" in the *Deutsche Rundschau*. It was suggested by the discovery in the previous year of a stone at Luxor by Wilbour, which stone mentions the seven years of want, and the attempt of one Chit-het to banish the calamity. Brugsch testifies to the historical correctness of the story as given in Genesis, identifying many names and places. He says the evidence is so conclusive that you could believe the writer of the story of Joseph "read his statements concerning the affairs of ancient Egypt from the very monuments themselves." Another instance is the discovery of Ur of Chaldees. The Bible student had long been told to find Ur at Oorfah, six hundred miles away, entirely beyond the land of Chaldea. But the Bible still taught that Ur was in Chaldea. It was overlooked because modern students forgot that the Persian Gulf has been filled up by the Euphrates through the centuries, and the ancient city which was on its coast is far inland. For years they looked in the wrong

place, but the discoveries by Lenormant and
Smith have identified Mugheir as the site of
the home of Tereh and Abraham. The assumptions of the scholars, based on insufficient conjectures, were wrong. The statements of Scripture, based upon the facts, were
accurate and correct. Thus does every new
item of actual history confirm the reliability
of the infallible record of Scripture.

VII.—The Book of Genesis.

So far as the Bible is concerned, the history of man, his creation and development, is linked with the story of his redemption. "The light of nature and the works of creation and providence are not sufficient to give that knowledge of God and of his will which is necessary unto salvation." Therefore we have the revelation of that divine will and the record of God's dealings with men in connection with the bestowment of this saving truth. The purpose to accomplish this result at once explains the fact that all matters external are only touched upon as they bear some relation to the history of man's redemption, and also explains the marvelous 'consent o al the parts," from Genesis to Revelation. Jus so, also, this purpose explains the character of the Pentateuch, and is the key to its unity of design and construction. The great subject of the Pentateuch is the establishment of the Hebrew theocracy. Its central point is the giving of the law at Sinai. All that goes before leads up to this, and that which comes after recounts the way in which Israel was schooled in that law until Canaan was reached.

The design of the Book of Genesis is therefore made apparent. It is intended to reveal the unfolding of the divine plan up to the time of the exodus. The charge of composite authorship has been made against Genesis as against no other book. The Elohist and Jehovist are certainly here, according to the critics, if nowhere else. But the coherency of the record, from first to last, is most marked. The plan of procedure is seen in the recurrence of the formula: "These are the generations." Ten times we have this expression, holding us to a special line of descent, according to the divine selection. A glance at the following table will show the significance of this plan:

i. 1-ii. 3..............General account of the creation.
ii. 4-iv. 26...The generations of the heavens and the earth.
v. 1-vi. 8...................The generations of Adam.
vi. 9-ix. 29................   "   "   " Noah.
x. 1-xi. 9.....The generations of the sons of Noah.
xi. 10-26...................The generations of Shem.

xi. 27–xxv. 11............The generations of Tereh.
xxv. 12–18................   "   "   " Ishmael.
xxv. 19–xxxv. 29......   "   "   "   Isaac.
xxxvi. 1–xxxvii. 1.....   "   "   "   Esau.
xxxvii. 2–1. 26..........   "   "   "   Jacob.

By a brief analysis of this table we discover some instructive facts. The initial chapter gives a general account of the creation. The critics would find the contents of the second chapter to be another contradictory account of the creation. But evidently this is not the purpose of the chapter. Its thought is that out of all this creation we have to do with man. That much of the general account which bears upon the need of a man to till the ground already covered with herb and plant is repeated, and a more special account of man's creation follows. From Adam Noah the main purpose is to show how the institution of salvation was made necessary by the fall and corruption of the race. In the tenth chapter the writer pauses to give that remarkable ethnological register of the families of men "after their tongues, in their countries and in their nations." Then we come to Tereh, and note that the name of Abraham does not appear in our table. It is a remarkable omission. Had that table been prepared at a period long after Moses, it is morally certain that the name of Abraham would have been there. But the laws of literary criticism point to this unexpected feature as the surer evidence of authenticity. Note, further, how Ishmael is dismissed with six verses, for Isaac is in the chosen line of descent; and then how but one chapter is devoted to Esau, while Jacob and his family are considered as the seed of the coming nation.

As you study this plan you will see how it draws you irresistibly to the time of Moses as the standpoint from which it was written. Whatever historic materials or patriarchal records may have been used, the fact becomes clear that this book was written to fit into the account of the exodus and that it looked forward from the time that Canaan was promised to Abraham, past the thralldom of Egypt, to the time of Israel's settlement in the land. In former chapters we have seen that the Akkadian account of the flood demonstrates the existence of a plain continuous story previous to the time of Moses. We also have the testimony of Dr. Brugsch Bey to the unbroken continuity of the story of Joseph. To turn from all these evidences of coherency and unity to the theory of the critics, with their analysis as presented in Dr. Bissell's edition of Genesis in colors, is to appreciate his quotation from Prof. James Robertson, who says the crying need of the time "is of a criticism that shall start by admitting that the writer possessed ordinary intelligence and knows fairly well what he is writing about."

The charge that Genesis has in it much unhistorical matter should receive some attention One ground for this charge is the assumption that the cosmogony of the book is marked like the traditions of all nations, with mythical statements. Touching the account of the creation, the reader is referred to a recent publication by Prof. James D Dana, of Yale University, entitled "Genesis and Science," in which he tells us that the conclusions on the last page of science are in such marvelous harmony with the statements on the first page of Genesis as to convince him that no man could have written them without having been divinely inspired. Touching the points which arise in connection with the account of the flood, the reader is referred to Prof. J. W. Dawson's recent book on 'Modern Science in Bible Lands," in which this eminent Christian scientist successfully repels attacks against the unscientific character of biblical statements when they are fairly understood. We have previously noted the complete vindication of the historic accuracy of the Egyptology of Genesis. Modern ethnologists are amazed at the profound research revealed in the tenth chapter, whose contents are verified by every established fact of ancient history. Modern linguists are finding, as Prof Max Mueller says, "the elements of the three mother tongues as they existed before their first separation," in the Sumerian writings unearthed in the ruins of Birs Nimrod the traditional tower of Babel Thus along many lines the student of Genesis finds reassuring evidence that the Word of God will keep abreast of all advancing thought, and under all the fires of whatever sort will shine with the unfading luster of the eternal truth

VIII.—The Book of Exodus.

In the Book of Exodus we touch the life of Moses. Naturally, we would expect to find in it a certain infusion of that peculiar evidence of personal knowledge which gives a living character to contemporaneous history. And this we do find. One of the most notable of all the commentaries on Exodus is that of Dr. Kalisch. He viewed Exodus as "forming the center of the divine revelation," and consequently as being "the most important volume which the human race possesses." As Dr. Kalisch brings the intimate familiarity of Jewish scholarship to the text, it is very suggestive to have him assert, as against the Jewish and Christian critics, that "we see the completest harmony in all parts of Exodus; we consider it as a perfect whole, pervaded throughout by one spirit and the same leading ideas."

The critics are on the ground, but the student who attempts to follow them with profit is in despair. At times they virtually repudiate their own theories. For instance, Knobel, DeWette and others assign Ex. i. 15-22 to the Jehovist, whereas the word Jehovah does not occur in the passage, while Elohim occurs three times. Then, chapters xxv. and xxviii. are ascribed to the Elohist, whereas Elohim is not found in them, and Jehovah occurs five times. Chapter iii. is called Elohistic, though Jehovah occurs twenty times and Elohim but seven. There is something hopeless about this. Another style of analysis is given us by Professor Driver, in his discussion of the Decalogue. He is considering the likeness of the text to that of Deuteronomy, and says: "It is an old and probable supposition that in its original form the Decalogue consisted merely of the Commandments themselves, and that the explanatory comments appended in certain cases were only added subsequently." For instance, the original Second Commandment would be: "Thou shalt not make to thyself any graven image." Professor Driver discusses the problem, and considers the probability that the appended comments were added after Deuteronomy was written.

He concludes thus: "On the whole, therefore, the more probable view appears to be that these clauses are in their original place in Exodus." On one page we are told this added comment is improbable, and on the very next page we are told it is probable.

The Book of Exodus reveals the clear purpose to show how Israel multiplied in Egypt until the time of Moses, to give an account of the circumstances in which the Israelites quitted Egypt, and to describe the giving of the law, together with the way the people entered upon the institutional life which centered about the tabernacle service. The narrative flows on without a break. There are some gaps, but because of the simple fact that nothing occurred which called for a place in the record. The critics object to this unity on the ground that the narrative has a decidedly sectional character. It is true that we have several sections which seem to be complete in themselves, and this is just what we might expect from a narrator who wrote the account of one act or scene in the drama at intervals as opportunity afforded. While these sections appear upon analysis, they betray no disjointed character, but preserve a continuous harmony. If, however, this arrangement had been made by a literary redactor of a later age, he would probably have omitted some of the repetitions and covered up the sectional points. The very character of the work indicates that we have it in its original form.

The critics further object to the Mosaic authorship of Exodus because Moses is spoken of in the third person, and because once or twice there are expressions complimentary to Moses, which they say he would not have written about himself. As to the first point, it is historic that Xenophon and Cæsar, in writing histories of which they were the heroes, both speak of themselves in the third person. But the important fact is that speaking of one's self in the third person was common in Egypt at that time Kings had their victories recorded thus, and people wrote their own epitaphs beforehand in the third person. What more need be said? As to the mention of a praiseful fact, as in xi. 3, we may say the wonder is that there is not more of it. The reference is, in fact, decidedly modest, and in addition the whole book strikingly reveals a deep spirit of humility and sense of unworthiness in Moses.

We have some important facts of a positive character which the Book of Exodus contributes. Canon Cook, in his appendix to Exodus in the Speaker's Commentary, has elaborately treated of the frequent occurrence in the book of Egyptian words and phrases. From thirty to forty such words occur in the first sixteen chapters. The writer shows evident familiarity with the Egyptian language. Not only so, but he reveals an intimate acquaintance with the climate, customs and products of Egypt, such as implies a long residence there. It takes years to possess accurate knowledge of habits, usages, religious ideas, etc. Moreover, every year is adding evidence to the correctness of Exodus in this respect. Of equal importance is the fact that this same writer reveals an equally perfect familiarity with the Sinaitic peninsula, with its vegetable and animal products, and its natural phenomena. That part of the book which refers to the sojourn is pervaded by a local coloring, an atmosphere of the desert, which has always made itself felt by every traveler who has explored that region.

This double character of the writer's knowledge of Egypt and the Sinaitic peninsula points to Moses, and to no one else, as the writer. It is simply inconceivable that some later writer should reveal these characteristics. He would never have appreciated the significance of Egyptian words in his narrative. If some later imaginary writer had lived in Egypt, it is too much to ask us to imagine him traveling the Sinaitic peninsula, infested, as it is to this day, with murderous bandits. There was no time between the exodus and the reign of Solomon when an Israelite would have been at all likely to possess such familiarity. But why need we argue further? The book, from first to last, reveals the living touch of the great leader of Israel. Moreover, it is Exodus which specifically mentions the fact that Moses was writing these things in a book: xvii. 14 and xxiv. 4. Both external and internal evidence are in harmony in pointing to Moses as the only man who fills all the requirements essential to the authorship of this book.

IX.—The Book of Leviticus.

The Book of Leviticus forms the center and heart of the five books of Moses. It contains the greater part of the Sinaitic legislation, from the time of the erection of the tabernacle, commonly termed the Levitical code. The integrity of the book is generally admitted Many critics who favor different documents in other parts of the Pentateuch, ascribe this part mainly to one writer, the Elohist. Others, however, bring their dissecting-knife here as elsewhere. Only one passage in the text might intimate a later date, namely, xviii. 28. But the context shows nothing unnatural in the tone of anticipation which is here presented. The expected possession of the promised land gives meaning to the whole history.

In the midst of the legislation we have a historical section, comprising chapters viii.-x., recounting the consecration of Aaron and his sons before the congregation. Some of the critics say this section is mythical because it records a miracle. Others say it was forged in order to support the authority of the sacerdotal caste. To such extremities are they driven to disprove it as contemporaneous history. It is absurd to suppose that one forging an interpolation to exalt the priesthood of a later day, would have pictured the priests who figured in the narrative as receiving the punishment of death because of their sins.

The book is full of traces of the Mosaic period. In the earlier chapters, when the priests are mentioned, Aaron and his sons are named. The tabernacle is the sanctuary and no other place of worship is anywhere mentioned. The Israelites are always described as a congregation under the command of the elders of the congregation. Everything has reference to life in a camp, and that camp in command of Moses. This is illustrated by the fact that the law touching the slaughter of the sacrifice in chapter xvii., which was for the camp, was amended in Deut. xii., in view of the permanent settlement in Canaan. Almost every line touches the age of Moses. Yet the critics would have us believe that these laws gradually came into the life and customs of Israel through long years of development. Such a slow growth would not reveal these distinctive historic settings which identify the receiving of the laws at the hand of Moses.

Moreover, some of the laws clearly find their explanation in certain Egyptian customs against which the Israelites are warned and commanded. This is specifically stated in chapter xviii., where reference is also made to Canaan. In the chapter on the recent discoveries from the monuments, we presented the conclusive evidence that a man like Moses would know much of the general character of Canaan as well as Egypt. Moreover, Israel is taught that it is because of their sins against God that the Canaanites are to be exterminated. Hence the significance of laws which take meaning in view of Egypt on one side and Canaan on the other. A particular instance of familiarity with Egypt is the hint at the Egyptian custom of marriage with sisters, a custom which stands alone among the prevailing habits of antiquity. Herodotus and Diodorus tell of other abominations among the Egyptians prohibited in this section.

Another set of laws point to a pre-Canaanite origin, namely, those in chapter xxv., which refer to the Sabbatical year and the year of jubilee. It seems that this law was never observed until after the captivity. We learn from 2 Chron. xxxvi. 21 that the years of the captivity betokened the purpose of God to honor the law which Israel had broken. After the captivity the law was religiously kept, as was the law touching idolatry. But it is perfectly apparent that such a law could not have been promulgated at any time between the settlement of the land and the captivity. Everything in the atmosphere of the life of Israel makes against such a possibility. The law is a part of that ideal state which was so fully elaborated by Moses when he was delineating the divine portrait for the chosen people. It is just such passages which are the basis of the authority for utterances of the prophets in condemnation of Israel's departure from the known laws of Jehovah. The previous existence of the law is necessary for an adequate explanation of the later history of its observance. Israel recognized one of their crying sins, in punishment for which they suffered captivity, to be the failure to keep this law. But there is no time at which the law could have been given, in the light of the history, except at the time of Moses.

We have touched here a fact of far-reaching importance. The whole Book of Leviticus is marked by a prophetical character. Its elaborate ritual is saturated with a spiritual significance. It was a shadow whereof the substance is Christ and his kingdom. No one can study the Epistle to the Hebrews without realizing this fact, and realizing also that the man Moses, and no one else, was the chosen servant of the God of Israel, through whom this ceremonial system was given to the people. The reference is as clearly to the historic Moses as to the historic Abraham or the historic Christ. We read in Heb. iii. 5, 6 (R. V.): "Moses indeed was faithful in all his house as a servant for a testimony of those things which were afterward to be spoken; but Christ as a son, over his house." It was a delicate thing to intimate even to Christian Jews that Christ was worthy of greater honor than Moses. They venerated him almost to idolatry as their deliverer, leader, lawgiver and advocate with God. The inspired writer of the Hebrews means to say that Christ is the Moses of the New Testament. Moses, with his marvelous gifts, was raised up and trained and called of God for his specific life work. The law was given by Moses, grace and truth came by Jesus Christ. The institutions of Moses were the scaffolding, those of Christ the finished fabric of religious truth The utterances of the prophets assume the pre-existence of the laws. They do not intimate a slow building of fragments of legislation into a code that found its compact form after most of the life of Israel had been spent. Instead of this, the Book of Leviticus breathes a constant spirit of prophetic anticipation of Israel's future development into greatness as these laws of God are honored and obeyed.

X.—The Book of Numbers.

The special problems which the critics have discovered in the Book of Numbers are numerous. As you study the criticisms however, you realize that many of them are not really directed against the authenticity of the book so much as against its credibility. Certainly some of them are efforts to disprove its divine inspiration. As in other sections of the Pentateuch, they draw the line at every point where the narrative recognizes divine intervention. For instance, DeWette says it is quite unnatural to suppose that Moses would have been willing to spend forty years in wanderings when he was so near to Canaan, and he takes offense at the statement that this wandering was a punishment for Israel's disobedience. Such rationalistic, destructive views are by no means infrequent among the critics. In view of this, it is disheartening to have our modern followers of the critics, who are still counted evangelical, constantly quoting these destructive rationalists from page to page as among the authorities whom we are to follow.

It will be possible, in the limit fixed for these chapters, only to mention the special points of discussion in this book There is a gap of thirty-seven years in the record, in which we have no mention of the doings of Israel, excepting the account of the rebellion of Korah and his coadjutors. Some critics say this proves that Israel did not remain forty years in the wilderness, while others say it proves that the record is incomplete. But we have already noted, in chapter vii., that it is the manifest design of the sacred narrative to record only the events which touch the development of the plan of redemption Hence the record passes over in silence the time in which the people destined to die are being supplanted by the next generation. They have no more place in the record. The critics have also made much of the several events which the record crowds into the fortieth year. Their difficulty rises out of the assumption that each event mentioned was finished before the next took place; but evidently nothing prevents some of them from going on simultaneously, in which case the difficulty quickly disappears.

The critics have made savage attacks upon the statistics in this book, the number of fighting men, the number of the congregation and the number of the first born. We refer the reader to Keil or Kurtz if it be desired to see how every difficulty that has been imagined may be fairly solved. We are further told that the marching of such a vast host of people could not have been accomplished as the record intimates. Of course, even the critics will not deny that Israel did actually travel from Egypt to Canaan, and that they must have marched in some fashion. The account of the use of the silver trumpets and the actual plans for order and regularity all point to just the modes of movement recorded. Then objections are made to the account of the setting apart of the tribe of Levi as betraying the marks of fiction But the clear refutation of this charge is in the undeniable fact that the cities of the Levites, whose distribution is mentioned in chapter xxxv., were actually occupied by that tribe from the beginning The critics claim a contradiction between iv. 2, 3 and viii. 24, referring to the proper age of Levites for duty. A moment's examination shows that the first refers to carrying the tabernacle, and the second to performing sacred functions in the tabernacle. The heavier task required an age of thirty years; the lighter duties simply required a certain maturity of twenty five years.

The episode of Balaam has naturally received considerable attention. It is true it has a distinct character. It is also true that these three chapters might be dropped out and the record would seem to be complete, just at that point, without the account of Balaam. To the critics this is all-sufficient ground for declaring it of a later and different source. But if the episode occurred then and there, the history is not complete without it. Moreover, while the record from chapter xxi. to xxv. would seem unbroken, if the intervening section was dropped, still we would be at a loss to understand the references to Balaam in chapter xxxi, unless we had this record. As to how Moses secured the material, we find in chapter xxxi. that Balaam was slain among the Midianites and his effects captured. It is by no means an unnatural supposition that in this way Moses came into possession of the facts, without having a special revelation. Very naturally the style and literary finish would be different when the writer turned from journalistic annals to such a theme, which must have thrilled his soul with its vision of the guidance of Israel's God. It must not be overlooked that the nations particularly mentioned in Balaam's prophecy belong to the Mosaic period. The Kenites later disappear entirely. Reference to Agag in xxiv. 7 does not, as claimed, necessarily point to the time of Saul, because it is proved to have been the standing title of the Amalekite princes, as Pharoah among Egyptians, or Cæsar among Romans.

We must now refer to the positive evidences of Mosaic authorship. The minute touches here and there point to a writer who had lived through it all, as in xi. 5. Some of the passages clearly belong to the Mosaic age Bleek conced s chapters i ii iii. iv. xix., and parts of vi. x xxi and xxxiii. Ewald agrees largely with this, and adds parts of x. and xx., frankly admitting that "at a much later period they could not have been attempted." Concerning the camping-stations in xxxiii, there is almost unanimous consent in attributing it to Moses As to the songs in xxi., Bleek, in his Introduction, says: "It is so absolutely against all probability that they should be the production of a later age that DeWette has acknowledged them to be of the age of Moses. If we find here songs which do not contain any reference at all to the circumstances of a later time, but are, on the contrary, full of features of individuality which are not otherwise intelligible, and are without meaning except in reference to circumstances in the time of Moses, it becomes highly probable that they were not only composed in the Mosaic age but that they were then written down, and have come down to us from thence." We also have in this book the evidence of intimate acquaintance with Egypt, as xiii 22. A striking instance of these Mosaic traces is found in the reference to the boundary of the land The mention of the Arnon as the boundary between Moab and the Amorites indicates a record written while the Israelitish army was still on the south bank of the river. Then the fact that the boundaries mentioned in xxxiv. do not exactly correspond with the land actually occupied clearly points to this chapter as written before the entrance into Canaan, for no later writer, after Israel failed to occupy all the land, would ascribe to them land which they did not possess.

The subject of possible interpolations at a later date is naturally suggested in this study, for several instances are asserted to be found in Numbers. The idea that Moses wrote the Pentateuch verbatim as we have it is not to be defended, and, of course, need not be. It is reasonably certain that he used materials which were at hand, and it is also reasonable to suppose that occasionally interpolations have found their way into the text in later years. The burden of evidence indicates that the Old Testament canon received its permanent form during the Persian period in the years extending from Ezra to Nehemiah. The transmission of the Mosaic writings for a thousand years by copyists in the schools of the prophets and elsewhere, would, not unnaturally, involve occasional marginal comments by the copyists, which comments would gradually creep into the body of the text. There were inspired men whom we may believe to have been moved at times to make such additions In chapter xii. 3, we have an instance in point. In chapter xv., verse 32 indicates that the incident mentioned was recorded after the wilderness journey, quite likely by Joshua who also probably wrote the account of the death of Moses at the close of Deuteronomy. (Josh. xxiv. 26) All such interpolations do not impeach the Mosaic authorship, and are entirely consistent with the belief that the whole was guarded by the Holy Spirit.

XI.—The Book of Deuteronomy.

The application of the name Deuteronomy to the fifth book of the Pentateuch is somewhat misleading, as it is apt to suggest that we have here either a second code of laws or a recapitulation of laws already given, whereas it is rather a summary of the most salient features of Jehovah's dealings with Israel and the commandments whose observance was of supreme importance when they were settled in the promised land. Many parts of the law already given are not mentioned, and few new laws are given. It is the personal and ethical rather than the political and official aspect of the law that is dwelt upon. In fact, the book consists of a series of sermons, having historical and legislative features, but being especially hortatory and revealing the subjective spirit of the author. This latter feature is in contrast to the previous books, in which the objective element prevails. The admonitions, appeals and warnings of Moses are enforced by constant references to the history and law of which they knew and possessed the records. The book closes with some account of the last days of Moses' life.

We noted in Chapter V. that this book has more direct references to Mosaic authorship than the other four. But the critics say it is quite impossible to believe that Moses could be the author, because there is such a marked difference of style from that found in the fragments which they concede to be Mosaic, and because we have here many of the same grounds for objection which they make against the Mosaic authorship of most of the Pentateuch in any part of it. When we ask the critics how we can set aside the direct testimony of the book itself, they are ready with the answer. It is the only answer possible to them, and it reveals their desperate determination to push their theory against all odds. They boldly tell us that the author of this book perpetrated a deliberate forgery, and assumed the name of Moses to give a color of consistency to his work. Of course they do this with soft words and tell us that notions of literary property were not very strict at that early day, and that such fictions were common among conscientious men.

But we ask the name of this forger who foisted his fraud upon Israel at some later date, and we are told it was the prophet Jeremiah! Think of this man of God, this preacher of righteousness, being accused of writing this book himself, or conniving with his cousin Hilkiah, and giving it forth as the book of the law found in the temple, accused of deliberately lending himself to falsehood and practicing an imposition upon the people in the name of God! This reproach which the critics cast upon the character of Jeremiah should bring shame to their cheeks and hot indignation from the heart of every lover of God's word. It is true that the writings of Jeremiah are marked by numerous and striking resemblances to passages in Deuteronomy. As a priest, Jeremiah would be occupied from his youth in the study of the law, and, when called to admonish Israel, nothing could have been more natural than to draw largely from these discourses of Moses. There are frequent quotations in Jeremiah from other books of the Pentateuch. Moreover, it must be noted that the agreements between Deuteronomy and Jeremiah are not so many as their differences, both in peculiarities of words and in much of the sentiment.

A part of this invention of the critics involves the notion that the book of the law which Hilkiah found in the temple during the reign of Josiah was not the entire Penta'euch, but simply Deuteronomy. But it is also called the book of the covenant, which identifies it with Exodus. The reasons given by the critics for their theory are quite insufficient. They say if the law had existed before this time, it is inconceivable that it should have been lost as the record intimates. But the deplorable idolatry that prevailed during the reigns of Manasseh and Amon, extending through half a century, is all-sufficient explanation of the fact that the Pentateuch was neglected and ignored and actually unknown, except in the ranks of the few faithful of the class of Jeremiah. Then they say the whole book could not have been read through in one day. But it is an assumption to assert that it was all read in one day. Last of all, the critics say that it is suspicious to have the book found just at the time when it was needed to assist the plans of the reformers, and that this coincidence points to the inference that the reformers made the book to suit the occasion! It is amazing beyond credence! Divine providence counts for nothing The religious enthusiasm and revival that marked Josiah's reign are not sufficient explanation for them. A time must be found for the later authorship of Deuteronomy or the theory of the critics will fail, and Jeremiah must be loaded with this charge of imposture, while his character as a prophet is impugned For if he could declare as from Moses what was his own, why should he not declare as from God what was simply his own? The critics who are anxious to minimize predictive prophecy will think this a very small matter; but it will not be so regarded by all who believe the prophet to be the medium of communication between God and man.

One of the fundamental errors of the rationalistic critics is in urging that the non-execution of a law proves that it did not exist. The critics seem to have forgotten the dark ages of Europe previous to the Reformation Their argument would prove that the New Testament did not exist in its present form, until Luther found a copy of it in a monastery library. Certainly the New Testament was largely forgotten and unknown, though it had been in existence more than a thousand years. The arguments of the critics would prove Luther the author of the epistles to the Galatians and the Romans. But the non observance of the teachings of Christ, fails to prove their non-existence. We are too near to them for that. The critics are dogmatic about the Old Testament, though they build largely on conjectures. There were rationalistic critics who tried to disprove the historic authenticity of the New Testament Gospels but they could not explain the figure of the apostle Paul going up and down the coasts of the Mediterranean founding churches and filling them with a faith that lifted heathenism off its hinges, and turned the faces of Christian nations yet unborn toward the light. Just so the historic figure of Moses moves through the atmosphere of Old Testament history. It is a consistent living portrait that could never have been patched together by hap-hazard hands. That portrait is possible only when painted from life.

The critics also assert that Deuteronomy contains several passages which point to a later origin. As in the preceding books, these passages permit of reasonable explanations. For instance, it is urged that the expression "beyond the Jordan" plainly indicates that the writer was on the west bank of the river. But this expression was the actual term given to that territory, and it could have been used just as Cæsar could write of Transalpine Gaul without being south of the Alps. Moreover, in a few instances there might have been interpolations.

We should note a few of the positive evidences of the Mosaic authorship of Deuteronomy. The aspect and attitude of the writer, both retrospective and prospective, are those of one in the position of Moses at the time immediately before the entrance of the Israelites into Canaan. There is not a hint of Jerusalem, or the temple, or the later life in the land. The principal foes are the Canaanites, who disappear from the record in the time of the judges. The vivid reminiscences of Egypt and experiences there as of recent occurrence point to Moses. Such a statement as that in chapter iv. 3, 4, is intelligible only as spoken to those who witnessed the incident mentioned. Moreover, we have frequent references in the earlier prophets. Those found in Amos and Hosea are especially significant because they were prophets of Israel rather than of Judah; for this fact indicates that the ten tribes recognized and reverenced the Pentateuch before the separation. But evidently it could not have attained to universal acceptance had it not been by long usage already established. In the Book of Kings we have references which prove that the book was known in the kingdom of Israel from the time of its establishment. Hengstenberg calls attention to the important fact that "the entire action and operation of the prophets in the kingdom of Israel is an inexplicable riddle if we do not assume the public recognition of the Pentateuch in this kingdom as its basis." He proceeds to show how the prophets, though very annoying to the kings at times, were ever recognized as having a certain authority, which can only be explained by the existence of the laws on which they grounded their censures of kings and people, standing as messengers of Jehovah and preachers of righteousness.

XII.—The Book of Joshua and the Term "Hexateuch."

The Jews were accustomed to separate the Book of Joshua from the Pentateuch The five books of Moses composed what they called the law. Joshua was grouped with Judges, Samuel and the Kings, composing the books known as the 'Former Prophets." Evidently this division has its primary explanation in the fact that Moses was identified in the Jewish mind with the Pentateuch The fact that the contents of Joshua had a close connection with the preceding record was no doubt fully recognized by the people, but more conspicuous than this relationship was the fact that the age of Moses stands out as peculiarly the age of the authoritative establishment of the people under the divine institutions received at the hand of their great lawgiver. Considered from another point of view, the Book of Joshua may properly be grouped with the Pentateuch, rather than the succeeding records. As a portion of the history, it fills out the account of the settlement in the promised land and if added to the five preceding books would make a group of six. It is because of this mode of grouping that we have the term "Hexateuch,' the six books composing what is frequently called the Book of Origins.

As might be expected, the Book of Joshua abounds in references to the law of Moses and to the instructions which he gave to Joshua as his divinely appointed successor in the work of completing the conquest and settlement of the land, and establishing among the people of Israel the worship and the laws of God. So completely is the book thus identified with the preceding records that the critics have been forced to the necessity of asserting that it also is of later origin and that it bears the same traces of composite structure which they claim to find in the Pentateuch. The salvation of the theory of the critics depends upon this disposition of Joshua, and the grouping which puts the six books together has come mainly through this claim that all six are of a later date than that assigned to them by tradition. As this claim bears a manifest relation to the Pentateuchal problem, it calls for brief consideration here.

Arguments akin to those already mentioned in the preceding chapters are offered by the critics to prove the later date of the Book of Joshua. For instance, it is urged that 2 Sam. i. 18 teaches that the Book of Joshua was not written earlier than the time of David, and, therefore, the mention of this book in Joshua is proof that Joshua also was not written earlier than David's time. But there is reason to believe that the Book of Jasher was a collection of national ballads, which received additions from time to time. In Josh. x. 13 the Syriac version calls it the Book of Canticles, and understands it to be a book of songs commemorative of the brave deeds of Israelite heroes. Jasher literally means "upright," and the name would be equivalent to the "Hero Book" of the nation. There are clear intimations to justify this explanation, and so we find reasonable explanations from first to last of the various discrepancies and traces of a later date which the critics claim to have found. An occasional instance may reasonably suggest an interpolation or inaccuracy in

The Book of Joshua.　89

transmission; but the substantial integrity of this book, as of the Pentateuch, remains vindicated by the scholarly opponents of the critics.

More serious are the charges that the Deuteronomist embodied the references to his own work in the Book of Joshua in order to facilitate the reception of his pretended laws of Moses. We might ask why he did not introduce more of them, had this been his purpose; but we are concerned about the vicious, repellant character of the theory which would build up the word of God upon a substratum of deliberate subtle deception. It is scarcely credible that evangelical Christians can calmly champion a theory which claims that the men who were "moved by the Holy Ghost," the Spirit of truth, were dominated at the same time by a cunning spirit of fraud and deception Equally destructive of our faith in predictive prophecy is the assertion that the statement in vi. 26 is not the record of an utterance by Joshua, but only the invention of a prophecy after its supposed fulfillment, as recorded in 1 Kings xvi 34. This is what Dr. Davidson tells us, and he simply makes the supposed later writer a designing imposter, who intended to palm off his work as of an earlier date, but who has been caught in his trickery by the astute, scientific research of the critics. But what of the inspiration of the Spirit of the living God in all this making of his Holy Word?

Against these destructive views, we have in this book also the clear traces of its early authorship. Joshua may have furnished some of its data in his records, and the facts that follow indicate that the book was written not many years after his death. There is an entire absence of any allusion to the later condition of Israel. The statement in xv. 63 points to a time before David, and that in ix. 27 shows that the place had not yet been chosen for the permanent altar of the Lord. The reference to the Canaanites in Gezer in xvi. 10 could not have been used after the time of Othniel. Moreover, when we turn to verbal criticism, we find the critics passing over phenomena which are quite too important to be ignored. In the Pentateuch there is but one form of the masculine and feminine of the personal pronoun of the third person. The feminine form first appears in Joshua. It is a striking instance of the gradual development of the inflexions of a language. So the archaic form of the pronoun "these" is frequent in the Pentateuch, but does not appear in Joshua. We may also ask, if the same redactor gave us the six books of the Hexateuch, why he always used a shorter form of "Jericho" in the Pentateuch and the fuller form in Joshua. We could multiply such evidences that the Book of Joshua has not come to us from the same hand that gave us the Pentateuch, but that it was written not many years later than the Pentateuch by one who was entirely familiar with the contents of the books of Moses and the historic details of the settlement in the land of Canaan.

The importance of this evidence is manifest. Since the critics fail to identify the authorship of Joshua with that of the Pentateuch, the keystone has failed from their arch, for Joshua makes necessary the previous existence of the Pentateuch The Jewish rabbis were quite as capable Hebraists as the modern critics. They realized that from the standpoint of literary criticism a line was to be drawn between Joshua and the books of Moses. They had a Pentateuch instead of a Hexateuch because of more fundamental points of separation than agreement. The historic connection has a continuous flow through all of the Scriptures. Above all is there the manifest power of the Spirit breathing upon the Word, and any theory which would simply vitiate the purpose and character of inspiration is inevitably doomed to fail of recognition in the evangelical ranks of the followers of Jesus Christ.

XIII. A Word About Alleged Errors and Existing Discrepancies.

The evangelical Christian Church looks upon Holy Scripture as the word of God written. In 2 Peter i. 19-21, we are taught that "we have also a more sure word of prophecy; whereunto ye do well that ye take heed, as unto a light that shineth in a dark place, ... knowing this first, that no prophecy of the Scripture is of any private interpretation. For the prophecy came not in the old time by the will of man; but holy men of God spake as they were moved by the Holy Ghost." We also have Paul writing, in 2 Tim. iii. 16, that "all Scripture is given by inspiration of God, and is profitable for doctrine, for reproof, for correction, for instruction in righteousness." Both of these passages refer to the Old Testament writings, and therefore they apply to the Pentateuch. In the light of these words of inspiration we approach the consideration of the subject of this chapter.

We all understand that the writers of Scripture, while they were inspired of God, were also marked by the conditions and limitations of humanity. Every divine revelation has been a manifestation or communication which has borne distinctive evidence of being accommodated to the finite weaknesses of men. We are not surprised, therefore, by the fact that after being transmitted by human copyists through centuries, the Scriptures contain discrepancies in the text. Indeed, when we consider the circumstances, and find that these discrepancies are very few and nowhere touch the vital truth of the Word, we can not but believe that God has directly aided man in the task of perpetuating the integrity of the Scriptures, "and by his singular care and providence, has kept them pure in all ages." The writer is of those who believe the existing discrepancies may be fairly and fully accounted for by the theory that they are due to mistakes made by the copyists.

In recent years a discussion has arisen touching this question of the discrepancies which exist in the various texts which we possess. Most students of Scripture explain them as the writer has just done. Some, however, contend that these errors probably existed in the original texts. The champions of this view are mainly the adherents of the higher criticism. Taken by itself, the question is not of such serious character as is sometimes urged. The validity of inspiration can not be impugned by any theory about the original manuscripts, because such theory can not carry us away from the text which we have. The writer agrees with President Patton, who says in his monograph on inspiration: "I must take exception to the disposition on the part of some to stake the fortunes of Christanity on the doctrine of inspiration. Not that I yield to any one in profound conviction of the truth and importance of the doctrine." Without admitting that the present discrepancies existed in the original text, we need not be greatly disturbed by the theory of their possible existence. God evidently deems the Bible as we now have it sufficiently pure for his purpose. Every day it proves to be the wisdom of God and the power of God unto salvation. The writer could believe it possible that God might have deemed sufficiently pure an original text like unto the one we have.

But the dangerous fact about this theory is that it does not stand by itself. If the inspiration of the writers of Scripture were not denied outright by some of the critics, we might rest somewhat complacent at the thought that the Holy Spirit permitted some human imperfections to appear in the original texts. But knowing how destructive some of the critics would be, we shrink from a theory that is clearly a step toward the naturalistic views which they espouse. The danger is in the tendency which this theory betrays. Some evangelical adherents of the higher criticism advocate a middle ground that mediates between the destructive rationalism of the extreme critics and those who hold to what they call the "iron-clad dogma of verbal inspiration and literalistic infallibility." But we answer that the situation does not demand such a middle ground. We believe, with Prof. W. J. Beecher, that the evangelical critics are making unnecessary concessions to the rationalists. We agree with Dr. S. J. McPherson's comment concerning the writer's beloved teacher, Prof. H. P. Smith: "He held that, while believing the Bible to be the word of God and the infallible standard of religious faith and moral conduct, he did not regard it as inerrant on all subordinate matters of science and history. I do not say that he was right in that opinion. He may, and I believe he will, turn out to be mistaken in it." Very few Christians advocate a mechanical theory of inspiration. The Scripture writers were not merely pens, but penmen. In so far, we stand this side of the extreme ultra-orthodox opinions of a few; but we can not see any fair demand which would lead us to take the first step toward naturalism.

The whole atmosphere of the Bible is marked by a guarantee of accuracy in the text Paul writes in 1 Cor. ii. 12, 13: "We have received not the spirit of the world, but the spirit which is of God; that we might know the things which are freely given us of God, which things also we speak, not in the words which man's wisdom teacheth, but which the Holy Ghost teacheth." Canon Farrar says that Paul's view of inspiration led him to make 'the words of Scripture co extensive and identical with the words of God'; and that "the controversial use which he makes of Old Testament passages attaches consequences of the deepest importance to what an ordinary reader might regard as a mere grammatical expression." Dr. Farrar cites in illustration the familiar instance in Gal. iii 16, where Paul argues from the singular rather than the plural form of the word "seed" in God's promise to Abraham. So when Christ said "It is written," the reader does not distinguish the particular utterance as more accurate than any other, but recognizes the force of the teaching to be an endorsement of the divine authority that rests in all the Old Testament. Moreover, such utterances from our Lord as "the Scripture can not be broken" clearly justify the inference that the slight discrepancies that now exist have crept into the text, and that the inspired writers gave us the word of God free from error.

While we have considered this subject somewhat in a general way, we have not forgotten its bearing upon our more special study of the Pentateuch. The "thus saith the Lord" which appears on page after page in connection with the person of Moses as God's spokesman to Israel, takes on peculiar significance in the light of the recognition which the New Testament constantly gives to the Pentateuchal passages. For it strikes at the very heart of the naturalistic theory that denies a substantial unity to the Mosaic writings, and would have us believe the present form of the book to be a compilation of fragments and documents edited long years after Moses, but in his name. The spirit of "pious fraud" which the critics must advocate to save their assumption is strangely at variance with the frank, clear, unsuspecting view which the God-inspired men of the Bible had of Moses and his book. Dr. J. J. Lampe makes a fair argument when he says: "It is well to notice, as a most eloquent testimony to the literal and complete inspiration of the written word of God, that whenever men have taken this book and have spoken from it with a 'thus saith the Lord,' they have touched the consciences of men, led them in faith and repentance to the Savior, turned the world upside down, banished innumerable wrongs and falsehoods, and renewed human society in a life of moral and spiritual beauty."

XIV.—Christ and the Critics.

What was the opinion of the Lord Jesus Christ concerning the Mosaic authorship of the Pentateuch? His opinion ought to be ours. Any teaching concerning the Pentateuch which is inconsistent with the divine instruction of Christ must be unhistoric and unscientific, as it is unscriptural. Moses is named eighty times in the New Testament, twenty-four times as the author, and fifteen times as the writer of the whole or a part of the law. We shall note especially Christ's own words. In Matt. xv. 1-9, and Mark vii. 1-13 we have the fifth commandment and the law which sentenced to death the man who cursed his parents ascribed indifferently to God and to Moses, and put in opposition to the commandments of men which had grown up by a course of traditions. So in Matt xxii., where the Sadducees were attempting to puzzle our Lord about the resurrection, Jesus said to them: "As touching the resurrection of the dead, have ye not read that which was spoken unto you by God, saying," etc.; or, as in Mark, "Have ye not read in the book of Moses;" or, as in Luke, "That the dead are raised, even Moses showed at the bush, when he calleth the Lord," etc., all three quoting from Exod. iii. 6.

So we might multiply references. Our concern, however, is with the theory by which the critics would explain away the natural conviction that Christ meant exactly what he said in these references to Moses. They tell us that the Pentateuch was commonly referred to as "Moses," just as the Psalms were known as "David." This of course is true, but when the critics tell us we have no more right to identify Moses with the Pentateuch than we have to identify David with the Psalms, we deny the statement very earnestly. We do this not only because the Scriptures identify Moses with the Pentateuch far more specially than they identify David with the Psalms, but also because the substantial Mosaic authorship of the Pentateuch is a far more important matter than the Davidic authorship of the Psalms. It is true that we do not know who wrote certain Old Testament books, and that we are satisfied to rest in the fact that some man was inspired of God to do it. But it is not a parallel case which we have in considering the authorship of the Pentateuch, for here we face the necessity of identifying the divine authority of the institutions of Israel with their origin. There is a vast distinction to be made between a collection of inspired devotional poetry, some parts of which may be anonymous, and the authoritative history of God's covenant relation to Israel established at the hand of a man divinely chosen and prepared to elaborate its condition and laws as a State.

The explanation which the critics give of Christ's attitude toward the Pentateuch vitiates the claim of Christ to be an authoritative teacher of infallible truth. They tell us that our Lord simply accommodated himself to the accepted notions of this time; that he was not here to teach higher criticism; that he quoted from the Pentateuchal books, as a saying of Moses, without meaning to affirm that they were actually written by him, but merely because these books were generally attributed to him. They tell us that Christ's concern was simply about the passage quoted, rather than about its author. But in our Lord's citations from the book of Moses, the point of vital importance is not primarily in the language of the passage, but in the authority of the utterance. It was essential to the validity of his argument that this citation should be from none other than Moses. His appeal is to the authoritative lawgiver of Israel. It is true that Christ was not given to the literary criticism of the Scriptures, but it is no less true that he was a teacher of the truth, and did not come to foster errors and give them countenance. It is incredible that Christ could have spoken as he did if he knew that the Pentateuch was floated into public acceptance by being falsely imputed to Moses long years after Moses lived.

To avoid this hurtful conclusion that Christ in no way referred to this literary fiction, many of the critics would have us believe that our Lord did not know any better, and actually supposed that Moses did write the Pentateuch when in reality it was the product of a later age, which was falsely imputed to Moses.

This we are told of him who said: "I am the light of the world: he that followeth me shall not walk in darkness;" "I am the truth," and of whom we are told that he 'needed not that any should testify of man: for he knew what was in man." Several evangelical critics join hands with the rationalists in this view. It is another step in the naturalistic tendency Dr. Briggs says: "Those who understand the doctrine of the humiliation of Christ and the incarnation of Christ, find no more difficulty in supposing that Jesus did not know the author of the Pentateuch than that he did not know the day of his own advent." There is in that statement evident reference to the theory of the Kenosis which teaches that in "emptying himself' Christ well-nigh, if not entirely, eliminated the divine nature from his incarnate person. But our symbols teach that "Christ, being the eternal Son of God, became man, and so was, and continued to be, God and man, in two distinct natures, and one person, forever" This definition of the incarnation is squarely against the theory of Christ's ignorance. The advocates of this theory build almost entirely on one verse of

Scripture (Mark xiii. 32), where Christ says of the time of his advent: 'Of that day and hour knoweth no man, no, not the angels which are in heaven, neither the Son, but the Father."

It may well be questioned whether the analogy of Christ's teachings will permit of such an interpretation as to require that this statement is a confession of ignorance To "understand the doctrine of the humiliation of Christ and the incarnation of Christ," as that doctrine is clearly taught in the word of God, is to understand that the God-man was very God and very man. As the world's Redeemer, Christ's representative function was twofold. He was at once God's representative among men and man's representative before God. When he stood as God's representative before men, he exercised every one of the prerogatives of his divine nature, commanding the elements, healing diseases, forgiving sin, raising the dead, and also speaking of past and future as one whose knowledge is omniscient. When he stood as man's representative before God he exercised only the prerogatives of his human nature. In the economy of the Godhead the eternal Son and Spirit are one with the Father in his counsels. The eternal Son, therefore, as God, knows the day of his second coming, but as the Christ, as the messenger from God to men, he did not possess this item of knowledge in that which he was to reveal from the bosom of the Father. Interpreting this utterance by the manifest purpose of Christ to be recognized as very God in the flesh, we must give it this meaning, and having denied the validity of the claim that Christ confessed ignorance at any point, we are prepared to go further and assert that the theory of his ignorance touching the very teachings of Scripture itself is utterly unworthy of the Son of God, whose claim to be the supreme teacher of God's truth to men would be wellnigh farcical were such ignorance possible.

This vicious theory involves not only the intellectual furnishing, but the moral nature of Christ. The argument assumes that he was actually in error when professing to teach truth. As Canon Liddon says: "Our Lord quotes Deuteronomy as a work of the highest authority on the subject of man's relations and duties to God Yet we are assured that in point of fact this book was nothing better than a pious forgery of the age of Jeremiah, if indeed it was not a work of that prophet, in which he employed the name and authority of Moses as a restraint upon the increasing polytheism of the later years of King Josiah. . . . If Deuteronomy is indeed a forgery, Jesus Christ was not merely ignorant of a fact of literary history. His moral perceptions were at fault. Before us is no mere question as to whether Christ's knowledge was or was not limited; the question is, whether as a matter of fact he taught or implied the truth of that which is not true, and which a finer moral sense than his might have seen to be false. The question is plainly whether he was a trustworthy teacher of religious no less than of historical truth. We have words of his own which prove how truly he made the acceptance of the lower portions of his teaching a preliminary to belief in the higher. 'If I have told you earthly things, and ye believe not, how shall ye believe if I tell you of heavenly things?' How indeed? If, when he sets the seal of his authority upon the writings of Moses as a whole, and upon the most miraculous incidents which they relate in detail, he is really only the uneducated Jew who ignorantly repeats and reflects the prejudice of a barbarous age, how shall we be sure that when he reveals the character of God, or the precepts of the new life, or the reality and nature of the endless world, he is really trustworthy, as an authority to whom we are prepared to cling in life and in death?"

This keen and forcible statement reveals the fatal extreme to which the logic of the theory of the critics must go. Kuenen is more destructive still. In his work on the Prophets he says: "The exegesis of the writers of the New Testament can not stand before the tribunal of science. We must either cast aside as worthless our dearly bought scientific method, or must forever cease to acknowledge the authority of the New Testament in the domain of the exegesis of the Old." That means, according to Kuenen, that we have no Christ and no Bible if we go the full length of the higher criticism. Those of us, however, who know of God's salvation in Christ will prefer to "cast aside as worthless" much of the product of the higher criticism and turn to Jesus Christ as our infallible guide As Dr. Lampe says: "He made it very clear, not only that he had a most minute and particular knowledge of all the events embedded in the Old Testament, and was perfectly familiar with the very spirit which actuated such men as Abraham, Noah, Moses, David and Isaiah—he was himself the subject of the Old Testament theophanies; commissioned the prophets to teach his truth in preparation for his coming and the confirmation of the gospel. They all taught and wrote by his Spirit, and it was a part of his mission to this world to fulfill every jot and tittle of all that was written in both the law and the prophets. It is impossible to believe that he did not know the time and the manner of producing the Old Testament books, all of which are so vitally connected with his mission."

The issue is vital and fundamental. We must choose between Christ and the critics. Do these modern critics understand the Scriptures better than Christ understood them? Think of a theory that brings us to such a question as this! Canon Liddon answers it in these words: "The man who sin cerely believes that Jesus Christ is God, will not doubt that his every word standeth sure, and that whatever has been sealed and sanctioned by his supreme authority is independent of, and unassailable by, the fallible judgment of his creatures concerning it."

XV.—Concluding Remarks.

The reader of the foregoing chapters will not fail to realize that in attempting to present in so brief a statement an intelligent idea of the views which are urged for and against the theories of the higher criticism, the writer has been compelled to omit much that might have been added. The purpose has not been to treat the subject comprehensively, and therefore only conspicuous features have been considered. The study of the individual books is intended to bring out the striking points, and in most cases the instances selected are among the most prominent about which there is contention. In accord with this principle, the Pentateuch has been selected, rather than other portions of the Old Testament, because its problem is the most important. A few remarks should be added in this concluding chapter.

Constant discrimination should be made between the legitimate methods of literary criticism and the unwarranted assumptions that mark the distinctive departures of much of the higher criticism Dr. Briggs says of such men as Drs. Green, Bissell and Osgood "They use the tools of criticism." This is true in that they are masters in the realm of the accepted laws of criticism which all students recognize, and of which the company of higher critics has no monopoly. But when Dr. Briggs says, "These three Americans have not yet won a single scholarly victory or checked for an instant the advance of criticism in America," he simply expresses his own opinion. Many will not agree with him. It is just because these and other leaders of the evangelical scholarship have faithfully defended the Scriptures against the assaults of many of the critics that the failure of the higher criticism is becoming apparent and a reaction is setting in against it, both abroad and in this country.

The critics lay the flattering unction to their souls that they are finding followers among men who, in reality, repudiate their claims. They mistake the toleration which would secure liberty of scholarship to all who hold to the essentials of faith in Jesus

Christ for an endorsement of their views. Dr Henry Van Dyke, in a recent sermon on "The Bible As It Is," gives expression to this spirit of toleration, but says: "As yet I have seen no good reason for thinking that Moses was not the author of the Pentateuch, although there are certain portions of it which he could hardly have written, for example the account of his own death and burial; and the prophecies of Isaiah seem to me to be well enough accounted for by the supposition of a single author with two different styles. These opinions may be due to ignorance; but many of the conclusions of the higher criticism present themselves to such literary judgment as I possess, in the same aspect of inconclusive dogmatism as the theories of those who would persuade us that the poems of Homer were written by another man of the same name, and that Francis Bacon was the author of Shakespeare's plays." Nothing could be more apt than the expression "inconclusive dogmatism" to describe so much of the assumption of the critics.

In science it is necessary to demonstration that when a law is believed to be established by a sufficiently wide induction, the process should be reversed, and the law being assumed true, must be applied to known facts to see if the results correspond to observation. This was Newton's method. But the so-called scientific laws of the critics have utterly failed to stand this test. These methods applied to historians like Motley or Macaulay would fail to assign the various portions of their history to sources from which they have avowedly obtained them. No more would those methods assign to Shakespeare and his contemporaries the various portions of the works known to have been written by them in common, as the play of Henry VIII. The laws of higher criticism would make it quite impossible for James Russell Lowell to have written all that we know came from his pen. What could be more diverse in style, thought and language than "The Biglow Papers" and "The Vision of Sir Launfal"? Yet they are from the same man, in spite of the fact that the laws of the higher criticism go to pieces on this rock. But if they fail in the case of authors whose work we know, and who wrote in our own language, how can they expect us to accept them when applied to writings centuries old, when a thousand helps to a perfect explanation of all the facts have irrevocably perished? Especially are we deterred from this in the case of the Holy Scriptures when the critics assume to assure us of instances of literary fiction and deception, about which they can only be guessing. In fact, the growing reaction against these extreme critical assumptions is simply the expression of the demand of true science.

Just here we touch a vital consideration. It arises in view of the claims of the evangelical adherents of this criticism They are grieved because their orthodoxy is suspected. They claim to adopt the principles of the higher criticism without accepting the destructive conclusions of the extreme rationalists. They count themselves misunderstood by many. It is unfortunate to have such misapprehension in any quarter. No lover of the truth desires to misjudge any man. The reason why the evangelical critics do not escape suspicion is, however, not far to see. They do not draw clean-cut lines between themselves and the rationalists They quote all classes of critics on the same page and make no distinction. They go part way and betray tendencies, which to many seem threatening More serious is the fact that some of them are decidedly nearer to the rationalists than they were five or ten years ago. The drift seems to be in that direction. Moreover, the extreme critics denounce the half-way men as holding an untenable place. It must follow that many will look with suspicion and fear upon the movement, especially as the evangelicals have made unnecessary and unscientific concessions to the extremists. If any one is to blame, it must mainly be the critics themselves.

Meantime, Bible students should bring not only the purpose to demand demonstration rather than assumption from the specialists, but also to bring open minds ready to receive any fair conclusion which safe scholarship may present. As has been said, literary criticism is not to be ignored. It has done marvelous things during this century in advancing a true knowledge of the Scriptures. The following statement from the writer's honored and revered teacher, the late Dr. L. J. Evans, is to the point: "I do not claim that all movement has been progress, or that every 'find' has been a gain. I am well aware that in biblical science, as in every science, there are rash speculations, unproved hypotheses, wild and dangerous vagaries. Some corners of the field are full of will-o'-the-wisps, illusive, unsubstantial, unsafe, gleaming, I fear, with a light that is not from heaven. I have nothing to say in behalf of a bald agnostic, materialistic naturalism, or of an arbitrary, capricious rationalism, which, with *a priori* dogmatism, denies the supernatural, belittles or expunges sin and salvation, eliminates out of history God's revelation of himself, evaporates out of the Bible its pneumatic inspiration, chops up its contents into lifeless fragments, and sweeps away book after book into the abyss of legend and myth. But, on the other hand, there are conclusions in this field which all whose judgment is worth anything are agreed in regarding as substantially established. We must reckon with these facts. We must take them into the account. We must assign them their true value." This graphic description of much of the higher criticism only confirms what has been stated in the foregoing chapters. As to the number of "established conclusions," all will not agree, but as to the necessity of faithful and scholarly consideration of all claims, none will question.

This spirit of fair inquiry the writer has desired to reveal in this brief statement of the subject from the standpoint of one who, while according recognition to the legitimate claims of criticism, is convinced that the higher critics have failed to eliminate Moses from the Pentateuch The reader will note that this has been the point of contention. We do not doubt that Moses used materials which were at his hand, and therefore critical analysis has grounds for noting different sources. Moreover, we have not objected to occasional interpolations or to a later editorial arrangement of the whole But our aim has been to show that the critics can not maintain their position in denying to Moses the supreme place in the substantial authorship of the book. We believe it to be fairly proved that the substance of the Pentateuch must have been in existence from the time of Moses, and that much of it points to Moses as its author, as to no one else. The internal evidence of the Pentateuch itself, the constant references of later Scriptures, the institutional life of Israel, the corroborations of the monuments, and the clear teaching of Christ and his apostles, all unite in making a cumulative argument, which results in conclusive demonstration of the substantial Mosaic authorship of the Pentateuch.

It is the writer's prayerful hope that this monograph may serve to stimulate somewhat the already increasing study of the word of God. There are those who love it with every fiber of every heart string, and who are ready to devote their lives to the end that it may be known and read to the uttermost part of the earth, as the power of God and the wisdom of God unto salvation. It has been subjected to the fiery tests of the crucible, but, like the burning bush which Moses saw, it can not be consumed, because Jehovah is in the midst of it. The divine life is its living spirit. "The words that I speak unto you," said Christ, 'they are spirit and they are life." The light of a blessed immortality shines from its pages upon the way everlasting. The knowledge of it shall one day fill the earth as the waters cover the sea. The glory of it shall be told when the hosts of the redeemed "sing the song of Moses the servant of God, and the song of the Lamb."

www.ingramcontent.com/pod-product-compliance
Lightning Source LLC
Chambersburg PA
CBHW020128170426
43199CB00009B/689